This book belongs to:

_____

ISBN 0-7683-2160-3

Compiled and illustrated by Kathy Davis
© 1999 Kathy Davis Designs
www.kathydavis.com
All Rights Reserved

Published in 2000 by Cedco Publishing Company.
100 Pelican Way, San Rafael, California 94901
For a free catalog of other Cedco® products, please write
to the address above, or visit our website : www.cedco.com

Printed in China

1 3 5 7 9 10 8 6 4 2

I warmly dedicate this book

to

⋅ Lorraine ⋅

– my touchstone, my true blue pal,

my trustworthy flag-bearer.

A more loyal friend I could never hope for.

FRIENDS are FLOWERS that Never Fade

a little book for friends, about friends, in honor of friends

by Kathy Davis

Cedco Publishing Company . San Rafael, California

Acknowledgements

First, I must gratefully acknowledge my dear friends who have inspired this book. In addition, thanks to the many voices of family and friends whose contributions made this subject matter come alive for me, in particular the Atkinson and Ronka families and the students and staff at Simmons School.

Lastly, this book would not have been possible without the time and talents of my exceptional staff, especially Jodi, Jen, Marge, and Katie. Please take a bow.

CONTENTS

A Note from the Artist

Friendship is a theme of such fondness for me. Although many things in our world must change, our true friends remain a constant presence in our lives... and thank goodness for that! Friends are always there for us — in good times as well as tough times — to listen, to care, to share, to lend support. Our friends get the real us — and the real us is just fine with them!

Friends are Flowers that Never Fade takes a look at friendship through a collection of art, quotes, ideas, and personal reflections. I had such fun interviewing friends, family, and students about their thoughts on friendship. These segments, called "My Friends Say," appear throughout the book. You'll read answers to questions such as "What was the most fun you've ever had with a friend?" and "What qualities in a friend are most important to you?" I think the responses will make you smile.

Everyone seems to relate to friendship. It is my hope that this little book will touch you and inspire you to do something nice for a friend...

♡ ... give a good hug

🖐 ... reach out to one in need

✉ ... send a card just to let them know you care

MISSING PERSON ... remember a long "lost" friend

📝 ... write a juicy letter

☎ ... call them just to say "hi"

📖 ... give them this book !!!

ENJOY !

Remember to be happy.
Be good to yourself.
And be extra-good to your friends.

All My Best!
♡Kathy

❀ Seeds of Friendship ❀
(what is a friend?)

Although "friendship" seems complicated to define, being a friend is based on the simplest of things...trust, caring, support, and sharing. In other words, a friend is someone who...

- makes you laugh when you are blue
- calls you with news that's too good to wait
- helps you when things go wrong
- understands what you're saying, even when you're quiet
- helps you to see things clearly
- helps you to be brave when you're afraid
- knows when to listen
- knows when to offer their "two cents"
- makes you feel safe
- respects your solitude when you need it
- makes ordinary things fun
- lends you a hand, or an ear, whenever you need one
- makes you feel you're "A-OK"
- gives reassuring hugs
- helps you with tough decisions
- goes to bat for you
- is always just a phone call away
- really cares
- is a reflection of you

What is a friend?

My Friends Say...

"A friend is someone who..."

... understands you.
Brett, age 12

... you can rely on in all situations.
Fred

... I can confide in.
Jen

... appreciates you just the way you are.
Peter

... knows your faults and likes you any way.
Nadia, age 16

... makes you laugh.
Katie, age 13

... gives a true reflection of you.
Helen

 ... shares with you.
Maggie, age 4

... gives you a comfortable feeling.
Wendi

... is just as excited about my dreams as I am.
Gail

... you can talk to about anything.
Mike, age 13

... sticks around no matter what and supports you through difficult times.
Katie A.

 ... I call when I have something too good to keep to myself.
Marge

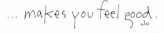

... plays a lot with you.
Gavin, age 7

... makes you feel good.
Jo

... you can laugh or cry with, and share joys and troubles.
Ruth

... you care about.
Sam, age 10

 ... you can trust.
KR

Friendship is a sheltering tree.

· Samuel Taylor Coleridge ·

꙳ True friendship is like sound health; the value of it is seldom known until it be lost. ꙳
Charles Caleb Colton

꙳ A friend is a present you give yourself ꙳
Robert Louis Stevenson

꙳ A friend is someone who understands your past, believes in your future, and accepts you today just the way you are. ꙳
unknown

꙳ Friendship is a single soul dwelling in two bodies ꙳
Aristotle

꙳ Love is rarer than genius itself. And friendship is rarer than love. ꙳
Charles Peguy

꙳ In my friend, I find a second self. ꙳
Isabel Norton

꙳ The better part of a man's life consists of his friendships. ꙳
Abraham Lincoln

 ꙳ Where your friends are, there are your riches. ꙳
German proverb

꙳ Friends should be preferred to kings ꙳
Voltaire

꙳ A little for you,
A little for me —
This is friendship. ꙳
Indian proverb

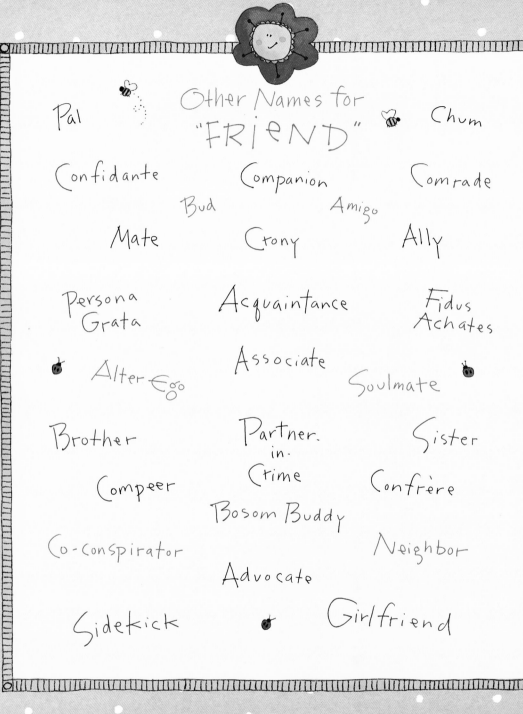

Other Names for "FRIEND"

Pal

Chum

Confidante

Companion

Comrade

Bud

Amigo

Mate

Crony

Ally

Persona Grata

Acquaintance

Fidus Achates

Alter Ego

Associate

Soulmate

Brother

Partner-in-Crime

Sister

Compeer

Confrère

Bosom Buddy

Co-conspirator

Neighbor

Advocate

Sidekick

Girlfriend

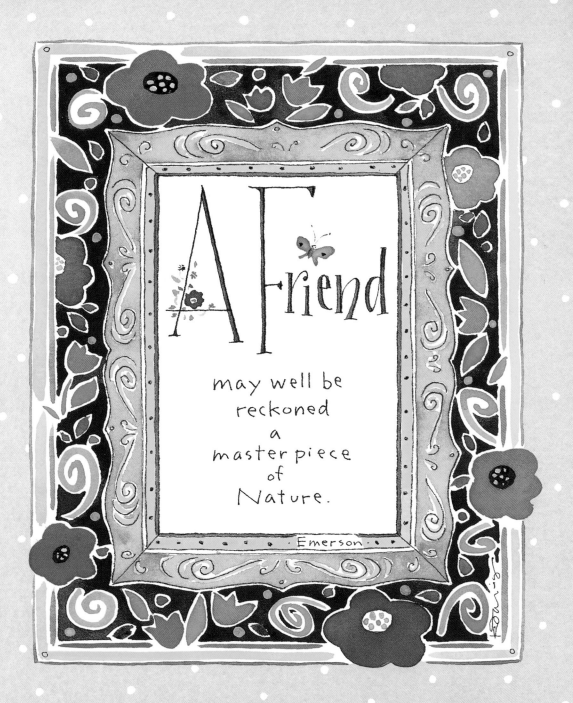

A Friend

may well be
reckoned
a
master piece
of
Nature.

Emerson

Friends are better than:

- cats, because they don't shed or scratch your furniture
- pieces of cake, because they don't make you gain weight
- mates, because they won't have lovers' quarrels with you
- parents, because they don't put you on guilt trips
- vacations, because they don't end too soon
- good workouts, because they don't make you sweat
- TV shows, because they don't break for commercials
- naps, because they don't leave you feeling groggy
- movies, because they don't make you wait in line
- comfy chairs, because they don't make you feel lazy
- books, because you don't have to worry about losing your place
- beaches, because you don't have to deal with the sand
- cars, because they won't run out of gas
- a box of chocolates, because you always know what you'll get
- dogs, because they don't usually slobber
- hot baths, because they don't put you to sleep
- pills, because they aren't hard to swallow
- ice cream cones, because they aren't drippy
- MOST everyTHING !!!

friend

One who knows
all about you
&
Loves you
just the same.

ELBERT HUBBARD

❧ Budding Friendships ❧
(making new friends)

❧ We cannot tell the precise moment when friendship is formed. As in filling a vessel drop by drop, there is at last a drop which makes it run over; so in a series of kindnesses there is at last a drop which makes the heart run over. ❧
James Boswell

How does friendship start? With a glance? A smile? A shared experience?

❧ Most smiles are started by another smile · ❧
Anonymous

There's nothing nicer than making a connection with someone new. Acquainting ourselves with a new friend allows us to develop a familiarity and caring for them. Like collecting treasures on a beach, we gather tidbits of information... what makes them laugh, their likes and dislikes, their history, fears, hopes, and dreams. Our new friends also awaken in us another aspect of ourselves. So, as we delight in the discoveries about our new friends, we also come to learn and appreciate more about ourselves —

a <u>double</u> delight!

❧ Like a butterfly emerging from its cocoon, a new friendship comes into its own full of promise and beauty. · ❧

10 Ways to Make a New Friend:

1. pay a compliment
2. listen
3. recommend a good book
4. ask their opinion
5. pick flowers for them
6. lend a hand
7. share common experiences
8. treat them to a soda or cup of coffee
9. commiserate with them
10. invite them to a movie

❧ Blessed are they who have the gift of making friends.... It involves many things, but above all, the power of going out of one's self, and appreciating whatever is noble and loving in another. · ❧   Thomas Hughes

·Don't walk in front of me·
I may not follow.

Don't walk behind me.
I may not lead.

·Just walk beside me·
and be
my
friend

·unknown·

If Friends were flowers

Rules of Friendship

DO's		DON'T's
Remember their birthdays		Rub in how old they are
Laugh with them		Laugh at them
Give advice when it's asked for		Say "I told you so" even if it's true
Compliment them on a new outfit		Buy the same outfit
Extend yourself with a favor		Make a big deal of it
Be willing to share your things with them		Lend them something if you really need it back
Tell them when they look good		Tell them they could lose a few pounds
Tell them your good news		Only talk about yourself
Feel you can ask for their help.		Ask them to help you move too many times.

What are the most important qualities in a friend?

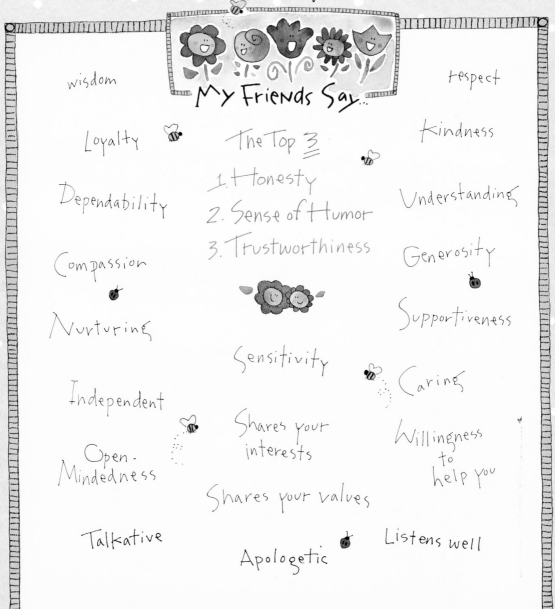

My Friends Say...

wisdom

respect

Loyalty

Kindness

Dependability

Understanding

The Top 3
1. Honesty
2. Sense of Humor
3. Trustworthiness

Compassion

Generosity

Nurturing

Supportiveness

Sensitivity

Independent

Caring

Shares your interests

Open-Mindedness

Willingness to help you

Shares your values

Talkative

Listens well

Apologetic

❊ Perennial Friends ❊
(keeping old friends)

> ❊ Make new friends, but keep the old. One is silver
> and the other gold. ❊
> *Girl Scout Song*

What could be more valuable than an old friend?! Our old friends know us so well... sometimes better than we know ourselves!! They are the most trusted, most dependable, most familiar of our friends. A shared history is rich with warm understanding and satisfying memories. Having seen us at our worst and best, our old friends accept us for who we are. They have outlasted old lovers... shared rites of passage... and are probably just as old as we are!! Nothing is better for the soul than spending time with an old friend.

> ❊ Forsake not an old friend, for a new one does not
> compare with him. ❊
> *Ecclesiastes 9:10*

> ❊ Wishing to be friends is quick work, but friendship is a slow-ripening fruit. ❊
> *Aristotle*

> ❊ The best mirror is an old friend. ❊
> *German proverb*

> ❊ It is one of the blessings of old friends that you can afford to be stupid
> with them. ❊
> *Emerson*

> ❊ Ah, how good it feels! The hand of an old friend ❊
> *Henry Wadsworth Longfellow*

> ❊ Old friends are the blessings of a long life. ❊
> *Scottish proverb*

Why are old friends the best friends?

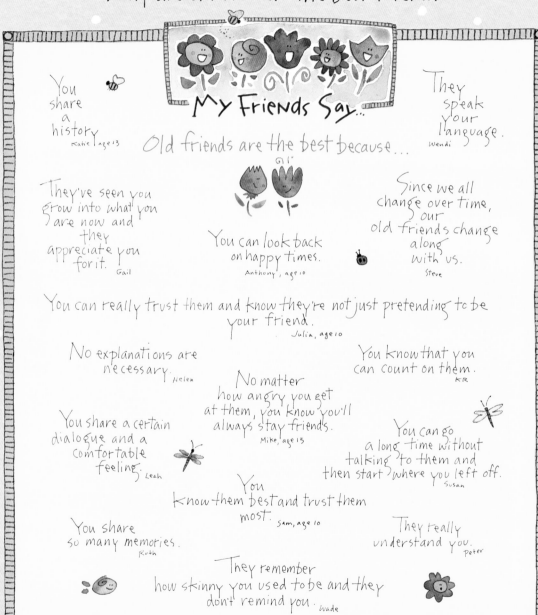

My Friends Say...

Old friends are the best because...

You share a history
Katie, age 13

They speak your language.
Wendi

They've seen you grow into what you are now and they appreciate you for it.
Gail

You can look back on happy times.
Anthony, age 10

Since we all change over time, our old friends change along with us.
Steve

You can really trust them and know they're not just pretending to be your friend.
Julia, age 10

No explanations are necessary.
Helen

You know that you can count on them.
KR

No matter how angry you get at them, you know you'll always stay friends.
Mike, age 13

You share a certain dialogue and a comfortable feeling.
Leah

You can go a long time without talking to them and then start where you left off.
Susan

You know them best and trust them most.
Sam, age 10

You share so many memories.
Ruth

They really understand you.
Peter

They remember how skinny you used to be and they don't remind you.
Wade

Nurturing Friendships
watering (caring & communicating)

Friendship is always a sweet responsibility... never an opportunity.
Kahlil Gibran

We need to take care of our friendships. Whether by simply staying in touch, remembering them at special times, or spending time together, our simple kindnesses show our friends that we care.

Nurturing far away friendships is easier than ever with e-mail, but don't forget cards, letters, calls, and visits !! Even when you occasionally fall out of touch with friends, it's amazing that when you do get together again, it feels like you haven't skipped a beat !!

We should not let grass grow on the path of friendship
St. Augustine

The road to a friend's house is never long

Short visits make long friends
American proverb

.: No love, no friendship can cross the path of our destiny without leaving a mark on it forever. :.
Francois Mauriac

.: Don't ever get so rich that you can afford to lose a friend. :.
unknown

.: The greatest acts of love are done by those who are habitually performing small acts of kindness. :.
unknown

.: A friend's eye is a good mirror. :.
Irish proverb

.: Whenever you part from your friend, you grieve not; for that which you love most in him may be clearer in his absence, as the mountain to the climber is clearer from the plain. :.
Kahlil Gibran

.: Happy is the house that shelters a friend. :.
proverb

.: "Stay" is a charming word in a friend's vocabulary. :.
Louisa May Alcott

.: Wherever you are, it is your own friends who make your world! :.
William James

Never shall I forget
the days which I spent with you...

Continue to be my friend,
As you will always find me yours.

·Ludwig van Beethoven·

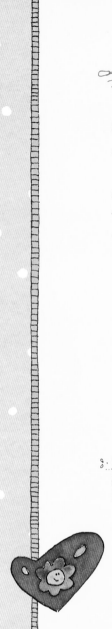

Weeding (helping in tough times)

When times are toughest, our true friends are there for us... no questions asked. Friends aren't there to judge us. They are there to support us.

At times we feel lost and we can't quite find ourselves, but somehow we can always find our friends. By listening to us, or just by being with us, our friends, in turn, help us to find ourselves once again! *whew! I knew I was here some place!*

The balm of life, a kind and faithful friend.
Arthur Quiller-Couch

What do we live for, if it is not to make life less difficult for each other?
George Eliot

A friend in need is a friend indeed
English proverb

It is my friends who have made the story of my life. In a thousand ways they have turned my limitations into privileges, and enabled me to walk serene and happy in the shadow cast by my deprivation.
Helen Keller

Friends show their love in times of trouble, not in happiness
Euripedes

If I can stop one heart from breaking, I shall not live in vain. If I can ease one life in the aching, or cool one pain, or help one fainting robin unto his nest again, I shall not live in vain.
Emily Dickinson

FRiENDS

NO MATTER WHAT

A friend

will joyfully sing
with you
when you are on the mountaintop,
and silently walk beside you
through the valley.

What's the nicest thing a friend ever did for you?

My Friends Say...

Baked fresh cookies for me.
Ruth

Visited me when I was sick.
Frank

Took me in to live with him when I needed it.
Peter

Sent me flowers on my wedding day.
Jen

Helped me feel better when I fell and hurt my chin.
Julia, age 10

Sent me a rose when I was feeling sad.
Susan

Called me when I was feeling down.
Jo

Stayed with my new baby and said, "Don't come back until you feel like it!"
Marge

Stuck up for me when others made fun of my new glasses.
Anthony, age 10

Brought me Jell-o when my wisdom teeth were taken out.
Nadia, age 16

Went out of their way to remember me on my birthday
Gail

Brought Get Well cards home from school for me when I was sick.
Jodi

Shared their dollhouse with me.
Maggie, age 4

Let me sleep over.
Emily, age 8

Took me to a baseball game.
Mike, age 13

Helped me when I was having problems.
Sam, age 10

You can do without people, but one has need of a friend.
Chinese Proverb

Friendship improves happiness and abates misery by doubling our joy and dividing our grief.
Addison

You do not really know your friends from your enemies until the ice breaks.
Icelandic proverb

No man is wise enough by himself.
Plautus

There are those who pass like ships in the night, who meet for a moment, then sail out of sight with never a backwards glance of regret; folks we know briefly, then quickly forget. Then there are friends who sail together through quiet waters and stormy weather, helping each other through joy and through strife. And they are the kind who give meaning to life.
unknown

I would not live without the love of my friends.
John Keats

No man can be happy without a friend, nor be sure of his friend till he is unhappy.
Thomas Fuller

Two are better than one, for if they fall, one will lift up the other.
Ecclesiastes 4:9-10

REAL
FRIENDS
believe
in
your
DREAMS

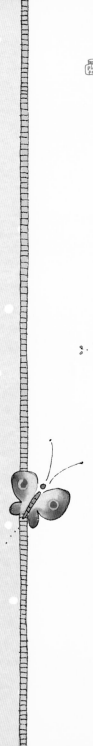

feeding (celebrating and giving)

The beauty of friendship is that it is unconditional in nature. But the very fact that we care about our friends means that we want to give to them. We want to share our fortunes and celebrate theirs. Celebrating special times, remembering birthdays, planning excursions, or simply sharing some good news are but a few ways friends give to each other. From the smallest kindness to the grandest generosity, our giving makes us feel so good.

No act of love, however small, is ever wasted.
Aesop

Your friend is your field which you sow with love and reap with thanksgiving.
Kahlil Gibran

I am wealthy in my friends.
Wm. Shakespeare

He that does good to another, also does good to himself.
Seneca

Treat your friends like family and your family like friends.
Cotton Mather

The best portion of a good man's life is his little, nameless, unremembered acts of kindness and of love.
William Wordsworth

"Give and take" -
good friendships make.
Scottish proverb

There are
    many people
    who come & go in our lives.

        A few
    touch us
    in ways
    that change us
        forever,

    making us better
    from knowing them.

    You have made a difference
        in my life,
        and for this
            I am grateful.

What is something nice you'd like to do for a friend?

My Friends Say...

Throw them a surprise party. Steve

Give them a carefree day. Helen

Help them with their kids. Susan

Buy them something nice. Katie, age 14

Visit with a friend who is in need. Ruth

Have them over for an old-fashioned outdoor tea party complete with big hats. Jen

Relieve a financial burden for them. Peter

Dedicate one of my paintings to them. Wendi

Write them a thank you note just for being a good friend. Jodi

Take them out to celebrate something. KR

Take them on a long, stress-free vacation! Leah

Be able to visit with a long lost friend. Frank

Help them if they hurt themselves. Gavin, age 7

Clean their house and make them dinner. Katie A.

Escape for a day together and spend non-hurried time. Marge

Do something that they wouldn't expect. Lorraine

I'd like to treat him the way he treats me. Anthony, age 10

Buy an extra-special toy for their birthday. Emily, age 8

Gift Ideas for Friends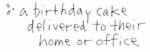

- a weekend away
- a handmade card
- bubble bath & scented candles
- enrollment in a class of their interest
- a balloon bouquet
- a poem you wrote (maybe even illustrated)
- a break from their kids
- a book you enjoyed and know they will
- tickets to a show, movie, circus, concert or lecture
- something that they can add to their collection

- a birthday cake delivered to their home or office
- a horoscope reading
- a day of golf, or shopping, or exploring
- a make-over
- a painting you created just for them
- an engraved friendship ring
- pet-sitting coupons
- a hot air balloon ride
- a homemade (or bought will do) frame with a special photo in it.
- birthstone necklace or earrings

- a spa gift certificate for a manicure, massage or facial
- a special souvenir from a place you visited
- a gift basket filled with things geared to their interests
- a flea market find that reminds you of them
- flowers from your garden
- something fancy to wear that they wouldn't buy themselves.
- homemade cookies or other items from your kitchen, with recipe attached - maybe in a hand-painted container

My
treasures
are my
Friends.

·Constantius·

:🌼 Blooming Friendships 🐝:
☺ (fun in the sun)

Chances are, you've shared your most fun times with friends.
Your friends usually share your same sense of humor, and
think you are a blast to be with! Whether it's sharing
laughs at parties, games, sporting events, travels,
shopping, or just hanging out, life's just more fun with
a friend.

: Shared joy is double joy and shared
sorrow is half sorrow. :
unknown

:Friends do not live in harmony merely, but in melody. :
Henry David Thoreau

: And the song from beginning to end, I found in the
heart of a friend. :
Henry Wadsworth Longfellow

: Treat your friends as you do your pictures, and place them in the
best light. :
Jennie Churchill

: The heart is happiest
when it beats for
others :
unknown

: One of the greatest pleasures
in life is conversation. :
Sidney Smith

: No toad is long
with good company :
Turkish proverb

: Together is the nicest place to be. :
unknown

What's the most fun you've ever had with a friend?

My Friends Say...

Playing ping-pong. Ruth

Singing Kareoke. Jen

Snorkeling in the Caribbean. Wade

Traveling through Europe together. KR

Having a water balloon fight. Jodi

Talking at sleep-overs. Katie

Trading POKÉMON cards. Gavin, age 7

When we got trapped in a parking garage. Helen

Staying at the pool all day long. Anthony, age 10

Having a great golf day together. Peter

Fishing. Brett, age 12

Sitting on a dock and talking about life's experiences. Steve

Trying on hats in a department store. Marge

Going on a trip to the shore. Lorraine

Playing ball together on a winning team. Frank

Taking a long road trip together. Katie

Visiting each other's houses and playing pool. Sam, age 10

Spotting deer from the back of a pick-up truck. Gail

Lying on the beach. Susan

Going to a baseball game. Emily, age 8

☺ Best Buds ☺
(the best of friends)

A best friend is truly a rare gem: the first one you
turn to with news — good or bad.... the one you trust
more than you trust yourself..... the one you can speak
to without saying a word .... the one who not only
recognizes and celebrates your good qualities but
accepts your shortcomings just the same.... the one
who is there for you — no matter what. A best friend
has lasting quality in a world where nothing seems to
last forever.

☺ My best friend is the one
who brings out the best in me. ☺
Henry Ford

☺ Two friends, two hearts,
with one soul inspired. ☺
Homer

☺ True friendship comes when silence
between two people is comfortable. ☺
unknown

☺ Oh, the comfort, the inexpressible comfort of feeling safe with a
person, having neither to weigh thoughts nor measure words, but
pouring them all right out, just as they are, chaff and grain
together; certain that a faithful hand will take and sift them,
keep what is worth keeping, and with the breath of kindness
blow the rest away. ☺ unknown

☺ My best friend is the man who in wishing me well, wishes it for my sake. ☺
Aristotle

☺ Hold a true friend
with both your hands ☺
Nigerian proverb

A TRUE FRIEND
is the
Rarest
of all Blessings.

· LA ROCHEFOUCAULD ·

What is the best thing about your best friend?

My Friends Say...

Her laugh
Emily, age 8

Her sincerity.
Ruth

He has the ability to forgive. Steve

She knows just what I am thinking. Helen

She teaches me to enjoy every single moment.
Leah

She never ceases to amaze me. Wendi

I know in my heart she will always be there.
Lorraine

She liked me enough to marry me. Peter

She always seems to be there to talk or go have coffee.
Jodi

She can laugh at our inside jokes.
Wade

I can confide in her and know she won't judge, criticize, or laugh.
KR

He's really kind and helps me.
Sam, age 10

She let me come play at her house.
Maggie, age 4

She would do anything for me and vice versa.
Gail

He's just like me!
Anthony, age 10

FAMOUS

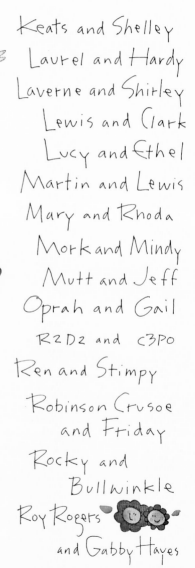

Abbott and Costello

Amos and Andy

Andy Griffith
   and Barney Fife

Batman and Robin

Beanie and Cecil

Bert and Ernie

Bob Hope and Bing Crosby

Butch Cassidy and
   the Sundance Kid

Cheech and Chong

Christopher Robin
   and Pooh

Dorothy and Toto

Fred and Barney

Garfield and John

Goofy and Mickey

Johnny Carson
   and Ed McMahon

Keats and Shelley

Laurel and Hardy

Laverne and Shirley

Lewis and Clark

Lucy and Ethel

Martin and Lewis

Mary and Rhoda

Mork and Mindy

Mutt and Jeff

Oprah and Gail

R2D2 and C3PO

Ren and Stimpy

Robinson Crusoe
   and Friday

Rocky and
   Bullwinkle

Roy Rogers
   and Gabby Hayes

FRIENDS :

Salem and Sabrina

Sherlock Holmes
and Watson

Snoopy and
Woodstock

Thomas Jefferson
and John Adams

Timmy and Lassie

Tom Sawyer
and Huck Finn

Tonto and
the Lone Ranger

Yogi and Boo Boo

 : Not Such Good Friends :

Betty and Veronica

Joan Crawford and
Bette Davis

George Washington
and Benedict Arnold

Sir Lancelot and
King Arthur

Itchy and Scratchy

Monica Lewinsky
and Linda Tripp

Marcus Brutus
and Julius Caesar

Anakin Skywalker
and Obi-Wan Kenobi

Romeo and Mercutio

∘⚬ Friendship Potpourri ⚬∘

Rose = Love

Ivy = Friendship

Rosemary =
  Remembrance

Fame is the scentless sunflower,
with gaudy crown of gold;
but friendship is the rose,
with sweets in every fold ∘⚬
Oliver Wendell Holmes

We can count on friendship to give a sweetness to our lives.
And there are as many different kinds of friends as
there are kinds of people. But one thing's for sure...
it's hard to beat the joys of friendship. We are truly
lucky when we can count friends among our many
⚬ blessings. ⚬

Gratitude preserves old friendships,
and procures new. ⚬
unknown

⚬ The language of friendship is not words, but meanings. ∘⚬
Henry David Thoreau

⚬ Good friends, good books and a sleepy conscience : this is the ideal life. ∘⚬
Mark Twain

⚬ Friends are not fickle,
Real friends are true.
And friends just don't come
Any better than you. ∘⚬

⚬ Life is nothing without friendship. ∘⚬
Cicero

⚬ I no doubt deserved my enemies, but I don't believe I deserved my friends ∘⚬
Walt Whitman

As for

Rosemary,

I lette it runne
all over my garden walls
not onlie because my bees love it,
but because it is
the herb sacred

·to·
Remembrance
and to
Friendship

Sir Thomas More

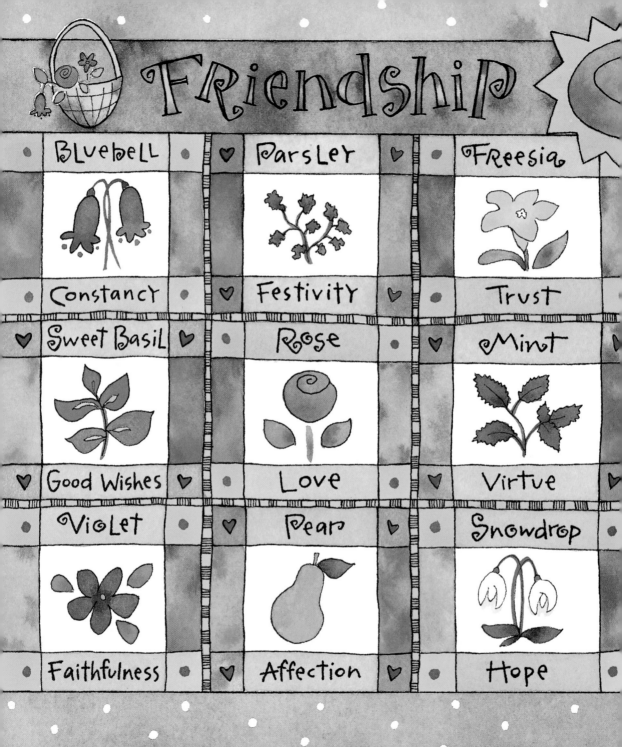

Friendship

Bluebell	Parsley	Freesia
Constancy	Festivity	Trust
Sweet Basil	Rose	Mint
Good Wishes	Love	Virtue
Violet	Pear	Snowdrop
Faithfulness	Affection	Hope

Garden

Jasmine	Strawberry	Larkspur
Grace	Excellence	Levity
Ivy	Pansy	Rosemary
Friendship	Warm thoughts	Remembrance
Carnation	Sweet Pea	Jonquil
Joy	Lasting Pleasures	Affection Returned

:6 SONGS about FRIENDS 8:
(titles & performers)

· Anytime You Need a Friend ·
Mariah Carey

· Bridge Over Troubled Waters ·
Simon & Garfunkel

· "Cheers" Theme ·
Gary Portnoy

· Circle of Friends ·
Edie Brickell

· Count on Me ·
Whitney Houston

· Friends in Low Places ·
Garth Brooks

· I'll be Your Friend ·
Amy Grant

· I'll be There for You ·
Rembrandts

· Lean on Me ·
Bill Withers

· Thank You for being a Friend ·
Andrew Gold

· That's What Friends Are For ·
Dionne Warwick (et al.)

· The Friendship Song ·
Fraggle Rock

· Wind Beneath My Wings ·
Bette Midler

· With a Little Help from My Friends ·
Beatles

· You've Got a Friend ·
Carole King // James Taylor

· You've Got a Friend in Me ·
Randy Newman // Lyle Lovett

:6 MOVIES about FRIENDS 8:

· Bad News Bears ·
1976

· Beaches ·
1988

· Butch Cassidy and the Sundance Kid ·
1969

· Circle of Friends ·
1995

· Driving Miss Daisy ·
1989

· Fried Green Tomatoes ·
1991

· Harry and Tonto ·
1974

· Harold and Maude ·
1971

· Homeward Bound ·
1993

· Melvin and Howard ·
1980

· My Friend Flicka ·
1943

· Now and Then ·
1995

· The Odd Couple ·
1968

· St. Elmo's Fire ·
1985

· Shawshank Redemption ·
1994

· Simon Birch ·
1998

· The Big Chill ·
1983

· The Breakfast Club ·
1985

· The Fox and the Hound ·
1981

· The Sunshine Boys ·
1975

· Thelma and Louise ·
1991

· Waiting to Exhale · 1995

· When Harry Met Sally ·
1989

❀ BOOKS about FRIENDS ❀
(titles & authors)

. A Friend is Someone Who Likes You .
Joan Walsh Anglund

. Adventures of Tom Sawyer .
Mark Twain

. Charlotte's Web .
E.B. White

. Corduroy
Don Freeman

. Divine Secrets of the
Ya Ya Sisterhood .
Rebecca Wells

. Do You Want to be My
Friend ?
Eric Carle

. How to Win Friends and
Influence People .
Dale Carnegie

. Girlfriends: Invisible Bonds, Enduring Ties .
Carmen Renee Berry and Tamara Traeder

. Of Mice and Men .
John Steinbeck

. Oliver Twist .
Charles Dickens

. Summer Sisters .
Judy Blume

. The Best Friends Book: true
stories about real best friends .
Arlene Erlback

. The Rainbow Fish .
Marcus Pfister

. The Three Musketeers .
Alexander Dumas

. The Velveteen Rabbit
Margery Williams

. (The Adventures of) Winnie the Pooh .
A.A. Milne

❀ TV SHOWS about FRIENDS ❀

. Adventures of
Timmy and Lassie .

. Ally McBeal .

. Barney and Friends .

. Bosom Buddies .

. Cheers .

. Ellen .

. Facts of Life .

. Friends .

. The Golden
Girls .

. Happy Days .

. The Muppet
Show .

. Our Gang .

. Rugrats .

. Seinfeld .

. Starsky and
Hutch .

. Thirtysomething .

. Three's
Company .

. Will and Grace .

Friendship Test
(20 ways to tell your real friends from imposters)

TRUE or FALSE .... Warning: false answers may indicate false friends

Real Friends...

1. ... don't call you COLLECT unless it's a true emergency.

2. ... understand you when others can't.

3. ... let you know if your slip hangs out, your zipper's down, you have salad greens stuck in your teeth, or you have toilet paper on your shoe.

4. ... really do want to watch your home movies.

5. ... tell you when they're worried about you.

6. ... find ways to stay in touch.

7. ... do not flirt with your significant other.

8. ... really listen and do not judge.

9. ... act like helping you out is no trouble ... even if it is.

10. ... will take care of your pet if the kennel's full.

11. ... do not say they'll call and then never do.

12. ... let you have the last cookie.

13. ... don't laugh at you when you tell them you want to be president, an astronaut, or a beauty queen.

14. ... are truly happy for you (never jealous).

15. ... do not compliment you without really meaning it.

16. ... accept you for who you are.

17. ... laugh at your stupid jokes cause they really think they're funny.

18. ... don't mind if you call them in the middle of the night (as long as it doesn't become a habit).

19. ... give from their hearts.

20. ... are still there when others have gone.

other books
by Kathy Davis
from Cedco Publishing

A Journal– <u>Friends</u> <u>are</u> <u>Flowers</u>
<u>that</u> <u>Never</u> <u>Fade</u> : <u>A</u> <u>Book</u> <u>for</u> <u>You,</u>
<u>from</u> <u>Me,</u> <u>About</u> <u>Us.</u>

<u>The</u> <u>Time</u> <u>to</u> <u>be</u> <u>Happy</u> <u>is</u> <u>Now</u>
a Book of Inspirations

An Address Book–
<u>The</u> <u>Time</u> <u>to</u> <u>be</u> <u>Happy</u>
<u>is</u> <u>Now</u>

When in the
Philadelphia area,
visit the original
Kathy Davis
retail store,
located in North
Wales.

Call (215) 661-8444
for information

Kathy Davis
COLLECTION

To order
Kathy Davis
products, visit our Online Store
at:
www.kathydavis.com
or call :
1·800·542·2797
for a
free catalog!

Help support
the following charities
by purchasing products from
our Online Store:

Lady Bird Johnson Wildflower
Center
www.wildflower.org

Buddy Dog Humane
Society
www.buddydoghs.com

Kathy Davis has always loved art. A former teacher, she designed her new career as an artist and writer one greeting card at a time. Her colorful style and uplifting messages now adorn thousands of products found worldwide. Kathy loves nature, and many of her designs reflect her favorite subjects of sunshine, flowers, and animals. Inspiration and humor often find their way into the original verse and quotations that adorn her creations. Kathy lives in the Philadelphia area with her family and a menagerie of pets.